READING LOG BOOK

I, _____
am the owner of this log book. The treasures
within are priceless.

Published by Kulhanjian's Notebooks & Journals a division of Las Vegas Book Company,
Las Vegas, Nevada, U.S.A

Designed by M. Mitch Freeland exclusively for Kulhanjian's Notebooks & Journals

Reading Log Book
8" x 10"

For information, contact: www.MMitchFreeland@gmail.com
www.MitchFreeland.com

First Edition Paperback: September 7, 2018

ISBN: 978-172012821-2

SPECIAL DISCOUNT SALES

Books published by Kulhanjian's Notebooks & Journals / Las Vegas Book Company are available at special quantity discounts worldwide to be used for training or for use in promotional programs, thoughtful gifts or for group engaged activities. Quantity discounts are available to Houses of Worship, study groups, corporations, educational institutions and charitable organizations.

Personalized front or back covers and endpapers can be produced in large numbers to meet specific needs.

For information, send us a quick email and tell us what you would like to do.

Email us at: www.MMitchFreeland@gmail.com

TABLE OF CONTENTS

Book Title	Date Recorded	Page

Books I Have Lent		96
Books I Have Borrowed		98
Books I Have Gifted		100
100 Books I want to Read		102
Books I Would Like to See on My Bookshelves		107

The books transported her into new worlds and introduced her to amazing people who lived exciting lives. She went on olden-day sailing ships with Joseph Conrad. She went to Africa with Ernest Hemingway and to India with Rudyard Kipling. She travelled all over the world while sitting in her little room in an English village.
—Roald Dahl, from *Matilda*

Book Title [   ]

Author: _____ Publisher: _____

Publishing Date: _____ Edition: _____

☐ Paperback ☐ Hardcover ☐ eBook ☐ Audio Book ☐ comb or spiral bound

Pages [_____]   ☐ Fiction / Fiction Genre: _____

                        ☐ Nonfiction ☐ Brand New ☐ Pre-owned

Book Category or Subject: _____

Book was first introduced to me by _____

Book was acquired from _____ on (Date) _____

Date Started_____ Date Finished _____

Why do/did I want to read this book?_____

The book made me feel.... ☐ Inspired ☐ Engaged ☐ Happy ☐ Grateful

☐ Enthusiastic ☐ Fearful ☐ Sad ☐ Depressed ☐ Angry ☐ Melancholy

☐ Surprised ☐ Enchanted ☐ Satisfied ☐ Empty ☐ Wiser ☐_____

What I learned from this book:

What I liked about this book:	What I did not like about this book:	*Reading a book on an airplane, on a ferry, on a bus, and on a train is always a disappointment—you arrive at your destination too quickly and with some regret.* —M. Mitch Freeland

Memorable Passages:

On a Scale of 1 to 5 stars I rate this book as a solid _____

I POSTED A REVIEW OF THIS BOOK

Date posted:_____

Posted on:

☐ Amazon ☐ Goodreads ☐ Barnes & Noble ☐ Smashwords ☐ Kobo ☐ Alibris ☐ eBay

☐ Other websites: _____

Review:

Book Title

Author: _____ Publisher: _____

Publishing Date: _____ Edition: _____

☐ Paperback ☐ Hardcover ☐ eBook ☐ Audio Book ☐ comb or spiral bound

Pages [_____]   ☐ Fiction / Fiction Genre: _____

☐ Nonfiction ☐ Brand New ☐ Pre-owned

Book Category or Subject: _____

Book was first introduced to me by _____

Book was acquired from _____ on (Date) _____

Date Started_____ Date Finished _____

Why do/did I want to read this book?_____

The book made me feel.... ☐ Inspired ☐ Engaged ☐ Happy ☐ Grateful

☐ Enthusiastic ☐ Fearful ☐ Sad ☐ Depressed ☐ Angry ☐ Melancholy

☐ Surprised ☐ Enchanted ☐ Satisfied ☐ Empty ☐ Wiser ☐ _____

What I learned from this book:

What I liked about this book:	What I did not like about this book:	If we encounter a man of rare intellect, we should ask him what books he reads. — Ralph Waldo Emerson

Memorable Passages:

On a Scale of 1 to 5 stars I rate this book as a solid _____

I POSTED A REVIEW OF THIS BOOK

Date posted:_____

Posted on:

☐ Amazon ☐ Goodreads ☐ Barnes & Noble ☐ Smashwords ☐ Kobo ☐ Alibris ☐ eBay

☐ Other websites: _____

Review:

Book Title

Author: _____ Publisher: _____

Publishing Date: _____ Edition: _____

☐ Paperback ☐ Hardcover ☐ eBook ☐ Audio Book ☐ comb or spiral bound

Pages [   ]   ☐ Fiction / Fiction Genre: _____

☐ Nonfiction ☐ Brand New ☐ Pre-owned

Book Category or Subject: _____

Book was first introduced to me by _____

Book was acquired from _____ on (Date) _____

Date Started_____ Date Finished _____

Why do/did I want to read this book?_____

The book made me feel.... ☐ Inspired ☐ Engaged ☐ Happy ☐ Grateful

☐ Enthusiastic ☐ Fearful ☐ Sad ☐ Depressed ☐ Angry ☐ Melancholy

☐ Surprised ☐ Enchanted ☐ Satisfied ☐ Empty ☐ Wiser ☐ _____

What I learned from this book:

What I liked about this book:

What I did not like about this book:

Books are the treasured wealth of the world and the fit inheritance of generations and nations.
— Henry David Thoreau, *Walden*

Memorable Passages:

On a Scale of 1 to 5 stars I rate this book as a solid _____

I POSTED A REVIEW OF THIS BOOK

Date posted:_____

Posted on:

☐ Amazon ☐ Goodreads ☐ Barnes & Noble ☐ Smashwords ☐ Kobo ☐ Alibris ☐ eBay

☐ Other websites: _____

Review:

Book Title [   ]

Author: _____ Publisher: _____

Publishing Date: _____ Edition: _____

☐ Paperback ☐ Hardcover ☐ eBook ☐ Audio Book ☐ comb or spiral bound

Pages [   ]   ☐ Fiction / Fiction Genre: _____

                           ☐ Nonfiction   ☐ Brand New   ☐ Pre-owned

Book Category or Subject: _____

Book was first introduced to me by _____

Book was acquired from _____ on (Date) _____

Date Started_____ Date Finished _____

Why do/did I want to read this book?_____

The book made me feel.... ☐ Inspired ☐ Engaged ☐ Happy ☐ Grateful

☐ Enthusiastic ☐ Fearful ☐ Sad ☐ Depressed ☐ Angry ☐ Melancholy

☐ Surprised ☐ Enchanted ☐ Satisfied ☐ Empty ☐ Wiser ☐ _____

What I learned from this book:

| What I liked about this book: | What I did not like about this book: | *So please, oh please, we beg, we pray, Go throw your TV set away, And in its place you can install A lovely bookshelf on the wall. Then fill the shelves with lots of books.* — Roald Dahl, in *Charlie and the Chocolate Factory* |

Memorable Passages:

On a Scale of 1 to 5 stars I rate this book as a solid _____

I POSTED A REVIEW OF THIS BOOK

Date posted:_____

Posted on:

☐ Amazon ☐ Goodreads ☐ Barnes & Noble ☐ Smashwords ☐ Kobo ☐ Alibris ☐ eBay

☐ Other websites: _____

Review:

Book Title

Author: _____ Publisher: _____

Publishing Date: _____ Edition: _____

☐ Paperback ☐ Hardcover ☐ eBook ☐ Audio Book ☐ comb or spiral bound

Pages [_____]   ☐ Fiction / Fiction Genre: _____

☐ Nonfiction   ☐ Brand New   ☐ Pre-owned

Book Category or Subject: _____

Book was first introduced to me by _____

Book was acquired from _____ on (Date) _____

Date Started_____ Date Finished _____

Why do/did I want to read this book?_____

The book made me feel.... ☐ Inspired ☐ Engaged ☐ Happy ☐ Grateful

☐ Enthusiastic ☐ Fearful ☐ Sad ☐ Depressed ☐ Angry ☐ Melancholy

☐ Surprised ☐ Enchanted ☐ Satisfied ☐ Empty ☐ Wiser ☐ _____

What I learned from this book:

What I liked about this book:	What I did not like about this book:	*All the computer can give you is a manuscript. People don't want to read manuscripts. They want to read books. Books smell good. They look good. You can press it to your bosom. You can carry it in your pocket.* — Ray Bradbury

Memorable Passages:

On a Scale of 1 to 5 stars I rate this book as a solid _____

I POSTED A REVIEW OF THIS BOOK

Date posted:_____

Posted on:

☐ Amazon ☐ Goodreads ☐ Barnes & Noble ☐ Smashwords ☐ Kobo ☐ Alibris ☐ eBay

☐ Other websites: _____

Review:

Book Title [   ]

Author: _____ Publisher: _____

Publishing Date: _____ Edition: _____

☐ Paperback ☐ Hardcover ☐ eBook ☐ Audio Book ☐ comb or spiral bound

Pages [   ]   ☐ Fiction / Fiction Genre: _____

☐ Nonfiction ☐ Brand New   ☐ Pre-owned

Book Category or Subject: _____

Book was first introduced to me by _____

Book was acquired from _____ on (Date) _____

Date Started_____ Date Finished _____

Why do/did I want to read this book?_____

The book made me feel.... ☐ Inspired ☐ Engaged ☐ Happy ☐ Grateful

☐ Enthusiastic ☐ Fearful ☐ Sad ☐ Depressed ☐ Angry ☐ Melancholy

☐ Surprised ☐ Enchanted ☐ Satisfied ☐ Empty ☐ Wiser ☐_____

What I learned from this book:

What I liked about this book:	What I did not like about this book:	*The love of learning, the sequestered nooks, And all the sweet serenity of books.* — Henry Wadsworth Longfellow

Memorable Passages:

On a Scale of 1 to 5 stars I rate this book as a solid _____

I POSTED A REVIEW OF THIS BOOK

Date posted:_____

Posted on:

☐ Amazon ☐ Goodreads ☐ Barnes & Noble ☐ Smashwords ☐ Kobo ☐ Alibris ☐ eBay

☐ Other websites: _____

Review:

Book Title [   ]

Author: _____ Publisher: _____

Publishing Date: _____ Edition: _____

☐ Paperback ☐ Hardcover ☐ eBook ☐ Audio Book ☐ comb or spiral bound

Pages [   ]   ☐ Fiction / Fiction Genre: _____

☐ Nonfiction   ☐ Brand New   ☐ Pre-owned

Book Category or Subject: _____

Book was first introduced to me by _____

Book was acquired from _____ on (Date) _____

Date Started_____ Date Finished _____

Why do/did I want to read this book?_____

The book made me feel.... ☐ Inspired ☐ Engaged ☐ Happy ☐ Grateful

☐ Enthusiastic ☐ Fearful ☐ Sad ☐ Depressed ☐ Angry ☐ Melancholy

☐ Surprised ☐ Enchanted ☐ Satisfied ☐ Empty ☐ Wiser ☐ _____

What I learned from this book:

What I liked about this book:	What I did not like about this book:	*I still love books. Nothing a computer can do can compare to a book.* — Ray Bradbury

Memorable Passages:

On a Scale of 1 to 5 stars I rate this book as a solid _____

I POSTED A REVIEW OF THIS BOOK

Date posted:_____

Posted on:

☐ Amazon ☐ Goodreads ☐ Barnes & Noble ☐ Smashwords ☐ Kobo ☐ Alibris ☐ eBay

☐ Other websites: _____

Review:

Book Title [   ]

Author: _____ Publisher: _____

Publishing Date: _____ Edition: _____

☐ Paperback ☐ Hardcover ☐ eBook ☐ Audio Book ☐ comb or spiral bound

Pages [   ]   ☐ Fiction / Fiction Genre: _____

☐ Nonfiction   ☐ Brand New   ☐ Pre-owned

Book Category or Subject: _____

Book was first introduced to me by _____

Book was acquired from _____ on (Date) _____

Date Started_____ Date Finished _____

Why do/did I want to read this book?_____

The book made me feel.... ☐ Inspired ☐ Engaged ☐ Happy ☐ Grateful

☐ Enthusiastic ☐ Fearful ☐ Sad ☐ Depressed ☐ Angry ☐ Melancholy

☐ Surprised ☐ Enchanted ☐ Satisfied ☐ Empty ☐ Wiser ☐ _____

What I learned from this book:

What I liked about this book:

What I did not like about this book:

To acquire the habit of reading is to construct for yourself a refuge from almost all the miseries of life.
— W. Somerset Maugham, in *Books and You*

Memorable Passages:

On a Scale of 1 to 5 stars I rate this book as a solid _____

I POSTED A REVIEW OF THIS BOOK

Date posted:_____

Posted on:

☐ Amazon ☐ Goodreads ☐ Barnes & Noble ☐ Smashwords ☐ Kobo ☐ Alibris ☐ eBay

☐ Other websites: _____

Review:

Book Title

Author: _____ Publisher: _____

Publishing Date: _____ Edition: _____

☐ Paperback ☐ Hardcover ☐ eBook ☐ Audio Book ☐ comb or spiral bound

Pages [   ]   ☐ Fiction / Fiction Genre: _____

☐ Nonfiction ☐ Brand New ☐ Pre-owned

Book Category or Subject: _____

Book was first introduced to me by _____

Book was acquired from _____ on (Date) _____

Date Started_____ Date Finished _____

Why do/did I want to read this book?_____

The book made me feel.... ☐ Inspired ☐ Engaged ☐ Happy ☐ Grateful

☐ Enthusiastic ☐ Fearful ☐ Sad ☐ Depressed ☐ Angry ☐ Melancholy

☐ Surprised ☐ Enchanted ☐ Satisfied ☐ Empty ☐ Wiser ☐_____

What I learned from this book:

What I liked about this book:	What I did not like about this book:	*Book collecting is an obsession, an occupation, a disease, an addiction, a fascination, an absurdity, a fate. It is not a hobby. Those who do it must do it.* — Jeanette Winterson

Memorable Passages:

On a Scale of 1 to 5 stars I rate this book as a solid _____

I POSTED A REVIEW OF THIS BOOK

Date posted:_____

Posted on:

☐ Amazon ☐ Goodreads ☐ Barnes & Noble ☐ Smashwords ☐ Kobo ☐ Alibris ☐ eBay

☐ Other websites: _____

Review:

Book Title [   ]

Author: _____ Publisher: _____

Publishing Date: _____ Edition: _____

☐ Paperback ☐ Hardcover ☐ eBook ☐ Audio Book ☐ comb or spiral bound

Pages [   ]   ☐ Fiction / Fiction Genre: _____

                         ☐ Nonfiction   ☐ Brand New   ☐ Pre-owned

Book Category or Subject: _____

Book was first introduced to me by _____

Book was acquired from _____ on (Date) _____

Date Started_____ Date Finished _____

Why do/did I want to read this book?_____

The book made me feel.... ☐ Inspired ☐ Engaged ☐ Happy ☐ Grateful

☐ Enthusiastic ☐ Fearful ☐ Sad ☐ Depressed ☐ Angry ☐ Melancholy

☐ Surprised ☐ Enchanted ☐ Satisfied ☐ Empty ☐ Wiser ☐ _____

What I learned from this book:

What I liked about this book:	What I did not like about this book:	*In the case of good books, the point is not to see how many of them you can get through, but rather how many can get through to you.* — Mortimer J. Adler

Memorable Passages:

On a Scale of 1 to 5 stars I rate this book as a solid _____

I POSTED A REVIEW OF THIS BOOK

Date posted:_____

Posted on:

☐ Amazon ☐ Goodreads ☐ Barnes & Noble ☐ Smashwords ☐ Kobo ☐ Alibris ☐ eBay

☐ Other websites: _____

Review:

Book Title [   ]

Author: _____ Publisher: _____

Publishing Date: _____ Edition: _____

☐ Paperback ☐ Hardcover ☐ eBook ☐ Audio Book ☐ comb or spiral bound

Pages [   ]   ☐ Fiction / Fiction Genre: _____

☐ Nonfiction   ☐ Brand New   ☐ Pre-owned

Book Category or Subject: _____

Book was first introduced to me by _____

Book was acquired from _____ on (Date) _____

Date Started_____ Date Finished _____

Why do/did I want to read this book?_____

The book made me feel.... ☐ Inspired ☐ Engaged ☐ Happy ☐ Grateful

☐ Enthusiastic ☐ Fearful ☐ Sad ☐ Depressed ☐ Angry ☐ Melancholy

☐ Surprised ☐ Enchanted ☐ Satisfied ☐ Empty ☐ Wiser ☐ _____

What I learned from this book:

What I liked about this book:	What I did not like about this book:	*No book is really worth reading at the age of ten which is not equally — and often far more — worth reading at the age of fifty and beyond.* — C.S. Lewis

Memorable Passages:

On a Scale of 1 to 5 stars I rate this book as a solid _____

I POSTED A REVIEW OF THIS BOOK

Date posted:_____

Posted on:

☐ Amazon ☐ Goodreads ☐ Barnes & Noble ☐ Smashwords ☐ Kobo ☐ Alibris ☐ eBay

☐ Other websites: _____

Review:

Book Title

Author: _____ Publisher: _____

Publishing Date: _____ Edition: _____

☐ Paperback ☐ Hardcover ☐ eBook ☐ Audio Book ☐ comb or spiral bound

Pages [_____]   ☐ Fiction / Fiction Genre: _____

                      ☐ Nonfiction ☐ Brand New ☐ Pre-owned

Book Category or Subject: _____

Book was first introduced to me by _____

Book was acquired from _____ on (Date) _____

Date Started_____ Date Finished _____

Why do/did I want to read this book?_____

The book made me feel.... ☐ Inspired ☐ Engaged ☐ Happy ☐ Grateful

☐ Enthusiastic ☐ Fearful ☐ Sad ☐ Depressed ☐ Angry ☐ Melancholy

☐ Surprised ☐ Enchanted ☐ Satisfied ☐ Empty ☐ Wiser ☐ _____

What I learned from this book:

What I liked about this book:	What I did not like about this book:	*A house without books is like a room without windows.* — Horace Mann

Memorable Passages:

On a Scale of 1 to 5 stars I rate this book as a solid _____

I POSTED A REVIEW OF THIS BOOK

Date posted:_____

Posted on:

☐ Amazon ☐ Goodreads ☐ Barnes & Noble ☐ Smashwords ☐ Kobo ☐ Alibris ☐ eBay

☐ Other websites: _____

Review:

Book Title [   ]

Author: _____ Publisher: _____

Publishing Date: _____ Edition: _____

☐ Paperback ☐ Hardcover ☐ eBook ☐ Audio Book ☐ comb or spiral bound

Pages [   ]   ☐ Fiction / Fiction Genre: _____

                           ☐ Nonfiction ☐ Brand New ☐ Pre-owned

Book Category or Subject: _____

Book was first introduced to me by _____

Book was acquired from _____ on (Date) _____

Date Started_____ Date Finished _____

Why do/did I want to read this book?_____

The book made me feel.... ☐ Inspired ☐ Engaged ☐ Happy ☐ Grateful

☐ Enthusiastic ☐ Fearful ☐ Sad ☐ Depressed ☐ Angry ☐ Melancholy

☐ Surprised ☐ Enchanted ☐ Satisfied ☐ Empty ☐ Wiser ☐ _____

What I learned from this book:

What I liked about this book:	What I did not like about this book:	*Books are the treasured wealth of the world and the fit inheritance of generations and nations.* — Henry David Thoreau, in *Walden*

Memorable Passages:

On a Scale of 1 to 5 stars I rate this book as a solid _____

I POSTED A REVIEW OF THIS BOOK

Date posted:_____
Posted on:

☐ Amazon ☐ Goodreads ☐ Barnes & Noble ☐ Smashwords ☐ Kobo ☐ Alibris ☐ eBay

☐ Other websites: _____

Review:

Book Title

Author: _____ Publisher: _____

Publishing Date: _____ Edition: _____

☐ Paperback ☐ Hardcover ☐ eBook ☐ Audio Book ☐ comb or spiral bound

Pages [_____]   ☐ Fiction / Fiction Genre: _____

☐ Nonfiction ☐ Brand New ☐ Pre-owned

Book Category or Subject: _____

Book was first introduced to me by _____

Book was acquired from _____ on (Date) _____

Date Started_____ Date Finished _____

Why do/did I want to read this book?_____

The book made me feel.... ☐ Inspired ☐ Engaged ☐ Happy ☐ Grateful

☐ Enthusiastic ☐ Fearful ☐ Sad ☐ Depressed ☐ Angry ☐ Melancholy

☐ Surprised ☐ Enchanted ☐ Satisfied ☐ Empty ☐ Wiser ☐ _____

What I learned from this book:

What I liked about this book:	What I did not like about this book:	*There are worse crimes than burning books. One of them is not reading them.* —Joseph Brodsky

Memorable Passages:

On a Scale of 1 to 5 stars I rate this book as a solid _____

I POSTED A REVIEW OF THIS BOOK

Date posted:_____

Posted on:

☐ Amazon ☐ Goodreads ☐ Barnes & Noble ☐ Smashwords ☐ Kobo ☐ Alibris ☐ eBay

☐ Other websites: _____

Review:

Book Title [   ]

Author: _____ Publisher: _____

Publishing Date: _____ Edition: _____

☐ Paperback ☐ Hardcover ☐ eBook ☐ Audio Book ☐ comb or spiral bound

Pages [   ]   ☐ Fiction / Fiction Genre: _____

☐ Nonfiction   ☐ Brand New   ☐ Pre-owned

Book Category or Subject: _____

Book was first introduced to me by _____

Book was acquired from _____ on (Date) _____

Date Started_____ Date Finished _____

Why do/did I want to read this book?_____

The book made me feel.... ☐ Inspired ☐ Engaged ☐ Happy ☐ Grateful

☐ Enthusiastic ☐ Fearful ☐ Sad ☐ Depressed ☐ Angry ☐ Melancholy

☐ Surprised ☐ Enchanted ☐ Satisfied ☐ Empty ☐ Wiser ☐ _____

What I learned from this book:

What I liked about this book:	What I did not like about this book:	*When I get a little money I buy books; and if any is left I buy food and clothes.* —Desiderius Erasmus

Memorable Passages:

On a Scale of 1 to 5 stars I rate this book as a solid _____

I POSTED A REVIEW OF THIS BOOK

Date posted:_____

Posted on:

☐ Amazon ☐ Goodreads ☐ Barnes & Noble ☐ Smashwords ☐ Kobo ☐ Alibris ☐ eBay

☐ Other websites: _____

Review:

Book Title

Author: _____ Publisher: _____

Publishing Date: _____ Edition: _____

☐ Paperback ☐ Hardcover ☐ eBook ☐ Audio Book ☐ comb or spiral bound

Pages [   ]   ☐ Fiction / Fiction Genre: _____

☐ Nonfiction ☐ Brand New ☐ Pre-owned

Book Category or Subject: _____

Book was first introduced to me by _____

Book was acquired from _____ on (Date) _____

Date Started_____ Date Finished _____

Why do/did I want to read this book?_____

The book made me feel.... ☐ Inspired ☐ Engaged ☐ Happy ☐ Grateful

☐ Enthusiastic ☐ Fearful ☐ Sad ☐ Depressed ☐ Angry ☐ Melancholy

☐ Surprised ☐ Enchanted ☐ Satisfied ☐ Empty ☐ Wiser ☐ _____

What I learned from this book:

| What I liked about this book: | What I did not like about this book: | *Be awesome! Be a book nut!*
— Dr. Seuss |

Memorable Passages:

On a Scale of 1 to 5 stars I rate this book as a solid _____

I POSTED A REVIEW OF THIS BOOK

Date posted:_____

Posted on:

☐ Amazon ☐ Goodreads ☐ Barnes & Noble ☐ Smashwords ☐ Kobo ☐ Alibris ☐ eBay

☐ Other websites: _____

Review:

Book Title

Author: _____ Publisher: _____

Publishing Date: _____ Edition: _____

☐ Paperback ☐ Hardcover ☐ eBook ☐ Audio Book ☐ comb or spiral bound

Pages [＿＿＿＿]　　☐ Fiction / Fiction Genre: _____

☐ Nonfiction ☐ Brand New ☐ Pre-owned

Book Category or Subject: _____

Book was first introduced to me by _____

Book was acquired from _____ on (Date) _____

Date Started_____ Date Finished _____

Why do/did I want to read this book?_____

The book made me feel.... ☐ Inspired ☐ Engaged ☐ Happy ☐ Grateful

☐ Enthusiastic ☐ Fearful ☐ Sad ☐ Depressed ☐ Angry ☐ Melancholy

☐ Surprised ☐ Enchanted ☐ Satisfied ☐ Empty ☐ Wiser ☐ _____

What I learned from this book:

What I liked about this book:	What I did not like about this book:	*What really knocks me out is a book that, when you're all done reading it, you wish the author that wrote it was a terrific friend of yours and you could call him up on the phone whenever you felt like it. That doesn't happen much, though.* — J.D. Salinger, *The Catcher in the Rye*

Memorable Passages:

On a Scale of 1 to 5 stars I rate this book as a solid _____

I POSTED A REVIEW OF THIS BOOK

Date posted:_____

Posted on:

☐ Amazon ☐ Goodreads ☐ Barnes & Noble ☐ Smashwords ☐ Kobo ☐ Alibris ☐ eBay

☐ Other websites: _____

Review:

Book Title [   ]

Author: _____ Publisher: _____

Publishing Date: _____ Edition: _____

☐ Paperback ☐ Hardcover ☐ eBook ☐ Audio Book ☐ comb or spiral bound

Pages [   ]   ☐ Fiction / Fiction Genre: _____

                    ☐ Nonfiction   ☐ Brand New   ☐ Pre-owned

Book Category or Subject: _____

Book was first introduced to me by _____

Book was acquired from _____ on (Date) _____

Date Started_____ Date Finished _____

Why do/did I want to read this book?_____

The book made me feel.... ☐ Inspired ☐ Engaged ☐ Happy ☐ Grateful

☐ Enthusiastic ☐ Fearful ☐ Sad ☐ Depressed ☐ Angry ☐ Melancholy

☐ Surprised ☐ Enchanted ☐ Satisfied ☐ Empty ☐ Wiser ☐ _____

What I learned from this book:

What I liked about this book:	What I did not like about this book:	*My Best Friend is a person who will give me a book I have not read.* — Abraham Lincoln

Memorable Passages:

On a Scale of 1 to 5 stars I rate this book as a solid _____

I POSTED A REVIEW OF THIS BOOK

Date posted:_____
Posted on:

☐ Amazon ☐ Goodreads ☐ Barnes & Noble ☐ Smashwords ☐ Kobo ☐ Alibris ☐ eBay

☐ Other websites: _____

Review:

Book Title

Author: _____ Publisher: _____

Publishing Date: _____ Edition: _____

☐ Paperback ☐ Hardcover ☐ eBook ☐ Audio Book ☐ comb or spiral bound

Pages [   ]   ☐ Fiction / Fiction Genre: _____

☐ Nonfiction ☐ Brand New ☐ Pre-owned

Book Category or Subject: _____

Book was first introduced to me by _____

Book was acquired from _____ on (Date) _____

Date Started_____ Date Finished _____

Why do/did I want to read this book?_____

The book made me feel.... ☐ Inspired ☐ Engaged ☐ Happy ☐ Grateful

☐ Enthusiastic ☐ Fearful ☐ Sad ☐ Depressed ☐ Angry ☐ Melancholy

☐ Surprised ☐ Enchanted ☐ Satisfied ☐ Empty ☐ Wiser ☐ _____

What I learned from this book:

What I liked about this book:	What I did not like about this book:	*In a good bookroom you feel in some mysterious way that you are absorbing the wisdom contained in all the books through your skin, without even opening them.* — Mark Twain

Memorable Passages:

On a Scale of 1 to 5 stars I rate this book as a solid _____

I POSTED A REVIEW OF THIS BOOK

Date posted:_____

Posted on:

☐ Amazon ☐ Goodreads ☐ Barnes & Noble ☐ Smashwords ☐ Kobo ☐ Alibris ☐ eBay

☐ Other websites: _____

Review:

Book Title [   ]

Author: _____ Publisher: _____

Publishing Date: _____ Edition: _____

☐ Paperback ☐ Hardcover ☐ eBook ☐ Audio Book ☐ comb or spiral bound

Pages [   ]   ☐ Fiction / Fiction Genre: _____

☐ Nonfiction ☐ Brand New ☐ Pre-owned

Book Category or Subject: _____

Book was first introduced to me by _____

Book was acquired from _____ on (Date) _____

Date Started_____ Date Finished _____

Why do/did I want to read this book?_____

The book made me feel.... ☐ Inspired ☐ Engaged ☐ Happy ☐ Grateful

☐ Enthusiastic ☐ Fearful ☐ Sad ☐ Depressed ☐ Angry ☐ Melancholy

☐ Surprised ☐ Enchanted ☐ Satisfied ☐ Empty ☐ Wiser ☐ _____

What I learned from this book:

What I liked about this book:

What I did not like about this book:

I don't believe in the kind of magic in my books. But I do believe something very magical can happen when you read a good book.
— J.K. Rowling

Memorable Passages:

On a Scale of 1 to 5 stars I rate this book as a solid _____

I POSTED A REVIEW OF THIS BOOK

Date posted:_____

Posted on:

☐ Amazon ☐ Goodreads ☐ Barnes & Noble ☐ Smashwords ☐ Kobo ☐ Alibris ☐ eBay

☐ Other websites: _____

Review:

Book Title [   ]

Author: _____ Publisher: _____

Publishing Date: _____ Edition: _____

☐ Paperback ☐ Hardcover ☐ eBook ☐ Audio Book ☐ comb or spiral bound

Pages [   ]   ☐ Fiction / Fiction Genre: _____

☐ Nonfiction   ☐ Brand New   ☐ Pre-owned

Book Category or Subject: _____

Book was first introduced to me by _____

Book was acquired from _____ on (Date) _____

Date Started_____ Date Finished _____

Why do/did I want to read this book?_____

The book made me feel.... ☐ Inspired ☐ Engaged ☐ Happy ☐ Grateful

☐ Enthusiastic ☐ Fearful ☐ Sad ☐ Depressed ☐ Angry ☐ Melancholy

☐ Surprised ☐ Enchanted ☐ Satisfied ☐ Empty ☐ Wiser ☐ _____

What I learned from this book:

What I liked about this book:

What I did not like about this book:

No book is really worth reading at the age of ten which is not equally — and often far more — worth reading at the age of fifty and beyond.
— C.S. Lewis

Memorable Passages:

On a Scale of 1 to 5 stars I rate this book as a solid _____

I POSTED A REVIEW OF THIS BOOK

Date posted:_____

Posted on:

☐ Amazon ☐ Goodreads ☐ Barnes & Noble ☐ Smashwords ☐ Kobo ☐ Alibris ☐ eBay

☐ Other websites: _____

Review:

Book Title

Author: _____ Publisher: _____

Publishing Date: _____ Edition: _____

☐ Paperback ☐ Hardcover ☐ eBook ☐ Audio Book ☐ comb or spiral bound

Pages [____] ☐ Fiction / Fiction Genre: _____

☐ Nonfiction ☐ Brand New ☐ Pre-owned

Book Category or Subject: _____

Book was first introduced to me by _____

Book was acquired from _____ on (Date) _____

Date Started_____ Date Finished _____

Why do/did I want to read this book?_____

The book made me feel.... ☐ Inspired ☐ Engaged ☐ Happy ☐ Grateful

☐ Enthusiastic ☐ Fearful ☐ Sad ☐ Depressed ☐ Angry ☐ Melancholy

☐ Surprised ☐ Enchanted ☐ Satisfied ☐ Empty ☐ Wiser ☐ _____

What I learned from this book:

What I liked about this book:	What I did not like about this book:	*When I was about eight, I decided that the most wonderful thing, next to a human being, was a book.* — Margaret Walker

Memorable Passages:

On a Scale of 1 to 5 stars I rate this book as a solid _____

I POSTED A REVIEW OF THIS BOOK

Date posted:_____
Posted on:

☐ Amazon ☐ Goodreads ☐ Barnes & Noble ☐ Smashwords ☐ Kobo ☐ Alibris ☐ eBay

☐ Other websites: _____

Review:

Book Title [   ]

Author: _____ Publisher: _____

Publishing Date: _____ Edition: _____

☐ Paperback ☐ Hardcover ☐ eBook ☐ Audio Book ☐ comb or spiral bound

Pages [   ]   ☐ Fiction / Fiction Genre: _____

                         ☐ Nonfiction   ☐ Brand New   ☐ Pre-owned

Book Category or Subject: _____

Book was first introduced to me by _____

Book was acquired from _____ on (Date) _____

Date Started_____ Date Finished _____

Why do/did I want to read this book?_____

The book made me feel.... ☐ Inspired ☐ Engaged ☐ Happy ☐ Grateful

☐ Enthusiastic ☐ Fearful ☐ Sad ☐ Depressed ☐ Angry ☐ Melancholy

☐ Surprised ☐ Enchanted ☐ Satisfied ☐ Empty ☐ Wiser ☐ _____

What I learned from this book:

What I liked about this book:	What I did not like about this book:	*Once you have read a book you care about, some part of it is always with you.* — Louis L'Amour in *Matagorda: The First Fast Draw*

Memorable Passages:

On a Scale of 1 to 5 stars I rate this book as a solid _____

I POSTED A REVIEW OF THIS BOOK

Date posted:_____

Posted on:

☐ Amazon ☐ Goodreads ☐ Barnes & Noble ☐ Smashwords ☐ Kobo ☐ Alibris ☐ eBay

☐ Other websites: _____

Review:

Book Title [   ]

Author: _____ Publisher: _____

Publishing Date: _____ Edition: _____

☐ Paperback ☐ Hardcover ☐ eBook ☐ Audio Book ☐ comb or spiral bound

Pages [   ]   ☐ Fiction / Fiction Genre: _____

                           ☐ Nonfiction ☐ Brand New ☐ Pre-owned

Book Category or Subject: _____

Book was first introduced to me by _____

Book was acquired from _____ on (Date) _____

Date Started_____ Date Finished _____

Why do/did I want to read this book?_____

The book made me feel.... ☐ Inspired ☐ Engaged ☐ Happy ☐ Grateful

☐ Enthusiastic ☐ Fearful ☐ Sad ☐ Depressed ☐ Angry ☐ Melancholy

☐ Surprised ☐ Enchanted ☐ Satisfied ☐ Empty ☐ Wiser ☐ _____

What I learned from this book:

What I liked about this book:	What I did not like about this book:	*A great book should leave you with many experiences, and slightly exhausted at the end. You live several lives while reading.* — William Styron in *Conversations with William Styron*

Memorable Passages:

On a Scale of 1 to 5 stars I rate this book as a solid _____

I POSTED A REVIEW OF THIS BOOK

Date posted:_____

Posted on:

☐ Amazon ☐ Goodreads ☐ Barnes & Noble ☐ Smashwords ☐ Kobo ☐ Alibris ☐ eBay

☐ Other websites: _____

Review:

Book Title [ ]

Author: _____ Publisher: _____

Publishing Date: _____ Edition: _____

☐ Paperback ☐ Hardcover ☐ eBook ☐ Audio Book ☐ comb or spiral bound

Pages [ ]   ☐ Fiction / Fiction Genre: _____

                 ☐ Nonfiction   ☐ Brand New   ☐ Pre-owned

Book Category or Subject: _____

Book was first introduced to me by _____

Book was acquired from _____ on (Date) _____

Date Started_____ Date Finished _____

Why do/did I want to read this book?_____

The book made me feel.... ☐ Inspired ☐ Engaged ☐ Happy ☐ Grateful

☐ Enthusiastic ☐ Fearful ☐ Sad ☐ Depressed ☐ Angry ☐ Melancholy

☐ Surprised ☐ Enchanted ☐ Satisfied ☐ Empty ☐ Wiser ☐_____

What I learned from this book:

What I liked about this book:	What I did not like about this book:	*I declare after all there is no enjoyment like reading! How much sooner one tires of anything than of a book! -- When I have a house of my own, I shall be miserable if I have not an excellent library.* — Jane Austen, in *Pride and Prejudice*

Memorable Passages:

On a Scale of 1 to 5 stars I rate this book as a solid _____

I POSTED A REVIEW OF THIS BOOK

Date posted:_____

Posted on:

☐ Amazon ☐ Goodreads ☐ Barnes & Noble ☐ Smashwords ☐ Kobo ☐ Alibris ☐ eBay

☐ Other websites: _____

Review:

Book Title

Author: _____ Publisher: _____

Publishing Date: _____ Edition: _____

☐ Paperback ☐ Hardcover ☐ eBook ☐ Audio Book ☐ comb or spiral bound

Pages [   ]   ☐ Fiction / Fiction Genre: _____

☐ Nonfiction ☐ Brand New ☐ Pre-owned

Book Category or Subject: _____

Book was first introduced to me by _____

Book was acquired from _____ on (Date) _____

Date Started_____ Date Finished _____

Why do/did I want to read this book?_____

The book made me feel.... ☐ Inspired ☐ Engaged ☐ Happy ☐ Grateful

☐ Enthusiastic ☐ Fearful ☐ Sad ☐ Depressed ☐ Angry ☐ Melancholy

☐ Surprised ☐ Enchanted ☐ Satisfied ☐ Empty ☐ Wiser ☐ _____

What I learned from this book:

| What I liked about this book: | What I did not like about this book: | *Books are the quietest and most constant of friends; they are the most accessible and wisest of counselors, and the most patient of teachers.*
 — Charles W. Eliot |

Memorable Passages:

On a Scale of 1 to 5 stars I rate this book as a solid _____

I POSTED A REVIEW OF THIS BOOK

Date posted:_____

Posted on:

☐ Amazon ☐ Goodreads ☐ Barnes & Noble ☐ Smashwords ☐ Kobo ☐ Alibris ☐ eBay

☐ Other websites: _____

Review:

Book Title

Author: _____ Publisher: _____

Publishing Date: _____ Edition: _____

☐ Paperback ☐ Hardcover ☐ eBook ☐ Audio Book ☐ comb or spiral bound

Pages [_____]   ☐ Fiction / Fiction Genre: _____

☐ Nonfiction ☐ Brand New ☐ Pre-owned

Book Category or Subject: _____

Book was first introduced to me by _____

Book was acquired from _____ on (Date) _____

Date Started_____ Date Finished _____

Why do/did I want to read this book?_____

The book made me feel.... ☐ Inspired ☐ Engaged ☐ Happy ☐ Grateful

☐ Enthusiastic ☐ Fearful ☐ Sad ☐ Depressed ☐ Angry ☐ Melancholy

☐ Surprised ☐ Enchanted ☐ Satisfied ☐ Empty ☐ Wiser ☐ _____

What I learned from this book:

What I liked about this book:

What I did not like about this book:

The man who is fond of books is usually a man of lofty thought, and of elevated opinions.
—John Dawkins

Memorable Passages:

On a Scale of 1 to 5 stars I rate this book as a solid _____

I POSTED A REVIEW OF THIS BOOK

Date posted:_____

Posted on:

☐ Amazon ☐ Goodreads ☐ Barnes & Noble ☐ Smashwords ☐ Kobo ☐ Alibris ☐ eBay

☐ Other websites: _____

Review:

Book Title

Author: _____ Publisher: _____

Publishing Date: _____ Edition: _____

☐ Paperback ☐ Hardcover ☐ eBook ☐ Audio Book ☐ comb or spiral bound

Pages [_____]   ☐ Fiction / Fiction Genre: _____

☐ Nonfiction   ☐ Brand New   ☐ Pre-owned

Book Category or Subject: _____

Book was first introduced to me by _____

Book was acquired from _____ on (Date) _____

Date Started_____ Date Finished _____

Why do/did I want to read this book?_____

The book made me feel.... ☐ Inspired ☐ Engaged ☐ Happy ☐ Grateful

☐ Enthusiastic ☐ Fearful ☐ Sad ☐ Depressed ☐ Angry ☐ Melancholy

☐ Surprised ☐ Enchanted ☐ Satisfied ☐ Empty ☐ Wiser ☐ _____

What I learned from this book:

What I liked about this book:

What I did not like about this book:

The reading of all good books is like a conversation with the finest minds of past centuries.
—Rene Descartes

Memorable Passages:

On a Scale of 1 to 5 stars I rate this book as a solid _____

I POSTED A REVIEW OF THIS BOOK

Date posted:_____
Posted on:

☐ Amazon ☐ Goodreads ☐ Barnes & Noble ☐ Smashwords ☐ Kobo ☐ Alibris ☐ eBay

☐ Other websites: _____

Review:

Book Title [   ]

Author: _____ Publisher: _____

Publishing Date: _____ Edition: _____

☐ Paperback ☐ Hardcover ☐ eBook ☐ Audio Book ☐ comb or spiral bound

Pages [   ]   ☐ Fiction / Fiction Genre: _____

☐ Nonfiction   ☐ Brand New   ☐ Pre-owned

Book Category or Subject: _____

Book was first introduced to me by _____

Book was acquired from _____ on (Date) _____

Date Started_____ Date Finished _____

Why do/did I want to read this book?_____

The book made me feel.... ☐ Inspired ☐ Engaged ☐ Happy ☐ Grateful

☐ Enthusiastic ☐ Fearful ☐ Sad ☐ Depressed ☐ Angry ☐ Melancholy

☐ Surprised ☐ Enchanted ☐ Satisfied ☐ Empty ☐ Wiser ☐ _____

What I learned from this book:

What I liked about this book:

What I did not like about this book:

The book salesman should be honored because he brings to our attention, as a rule, the very books we needed most and neglect most.
—Confucius

Memorable Passages:

On a Scale of 1 to 5 stars I rate this book as a solid _____

I POSTED A REVIEW OF THIS BOOK

Date posted:_____
Posted on:

☐ Amazon ☐ Goodreads ☐ Barnes & Noble ☐ Smashwords ☐ Kobo ☐ Alibris ☐ eBay

☐ Other websites: _____

Review:

Book Title

Author: _____ Publisher: _____

Publishing Date: _____ Edition: _____

☐ Paperback ☐ Hardcover ☐ eBook ☐ Audio Book ☐ comb or spiral bound

Pages [   ]   ☐ Fiction / Fiction Genre: _____

                        ☐ Nonfiction   ☐ Brand New   ☐ Pre-owned

Book Category or Subject: _____

Book was first introduced to me by _____

Book was acquired from _____ on (Date) _____

Date Started_____ Date Finished _____

Why do/did I want to read this book?_____

The book made me feel.... ☐ Inspired ☐ Engaged ☐ Happy ☐ Grateful

☐ Enthusiastic ☐ Fearful ☐ Sad ☐ Depressed ☐ Angry ☐ Melancholy

☐ Surprised ☐ Enchanted ☐ Satisfied ☐ Empty ☐ Wiser ☐ _____

What I learned from this book:

What I liked about this book:	What I did not like about this book:	*I find television very educating. Every time somebody turns on the set, I go into the other room and read a book.* — Groucho Marx

Memorable Passages:

On a Scale of 1 to 5 stars I rate this book as a solid _____

I POSTED A REVIEW OF THIS BOOK

Date posted:_____

Posted on:

☐ Amazon ☐ Goodreads ☐ Barnes & Noble ☐ Smashwords ☐ Kobo ☐ Alibris ☐ eBay

☐ Other websites: _____

Review:

Book Title [   ]

Author: _____ Publisher: _____

Publishing Date: _____ Edition: _____

☐ Paperback ☐ Hardcover ☐ eBook ☐ Audio Book ☐ comb or spiral bound

Pages [   ]   ☐ Fiction / Fiction Genre: _____

☐ Nonfiction   ☐ Brand New   ☐ Pre-owned

Book Category or Subject: _____

Book was first introduced to me by _____

Book was acquired from _____ on (Date) _____

Date Started_____ Date Finished _____

Why do/did I want to read this book?_____

The book made me feel.... ☐ Inspired ☐ Engaged ☐ Happy ☐ Grateful

☐ Enthusiastic ☐ Fearful ☐ Sad ☐ Depressed ☐ Angry ☐ Melancholy

☐ Surprised ☐ Enchanted ☐ Satisfied ☐ Empty ☐ Wiser ☐ _____

What I learned from this book:

What I liked about this book:

What I did not like about this book:

There is more treasure in books than in all the pirate's loot on Treasure Island.
—Walt Disney

Memorable Passages:

On a Scale of 1 to 5 stars I rate this book as a solid _____

I POSTED A REVIEW OF THIS BOOK

Date posted:_____

Posted on:

☐ Amazon ☐ Goodreads ☐ Barnes & Noble ☐ Smashwords ☐ Kobo ☐ Alibris ☐ eBay

☐ Other websites: _____

Review:

Book Title

Author: _____ Publisher: _____

Publishing Date: _____ Edition: _____

☐ Paperback ☐ Hardcover ☐ eBook ☐ Audio Book ☐ comb or spiral bound

Pages [_____]   ☐ Fiction / Fiction Genre: _____

                     ☐ Nonfiction   ☐ Brand New   ☐ Pre-owned

Book Category or Subject: _____

Book was first introduced to me by _____

Book was acquired from _____ on (Date) _____

Date Started_____ Date Finished _____

Why do/did I want to read this book?_____

The book made me feel.... ☐ Inspired ☐ Engaged ☐ Happy ☐ Grateful

☐ Enthusiastic ☐ Fearful ☐ Sad ☐ Depressed ☐ Angry ☐ Melancholy

☐ Surprised ☐ Enchanted ☐ Satisfied ☐ Empty ☐ Wiser ☐ _____

What I learned from this book:

What I liked about this book:

What I did not like about this book:

I cannot live without books.
—Thomas Jefferson

Memorable Passages:

On a Scale of 1 to 5 stars I rate this book as a solid _____

I POSTED A REVIEW OF THIS BOOK

Date posted:_____
Posted on:

☐ Amazon ☐ Goodreads ☐ Barnes & Noble ☐ Smashwords ☐ Kobo ☐ Alibris ☐ eBay

☐ Other websites: _____

Review:

Book Title

Author: _____ Publisher: _____

Publishing Date: _____ Edition: _____

☐ Paperback ☐ Hardcover ☐ eBook ☐ Audio Book ☐ comb or spiral bound

Pages [   ]   ☐ Fiction / Fiction Genre: _____

☐ Nonfiction ☐ Brand New ☐ Pre-owned

Book Category or Subject: _____

Book was first introduced to me by _____

Book was acquired from _____ on (Date) _____

Date Started_____ Date Finished _____

Why do/did I want to read this book?_____

The book made me feel.... ☐ Inspired ☐ Engaged ☐ Happy ☐ Grateful

☐ Enthusiastic ☐ Fearful ☐ Sad ☐ Depressed ☐ Angry ☐ Melancholy

☐ Surprised ☐ Enchanted ☐ Satisfied ☐ Empty ☐ Wiser ☐ _____

What I learned from this book:

What I liked about this book:	What I did not like about this book:	*The person, be it gentleman or lady, who has not pleasure in a good novel, must be intolerably stupid.* — Jane Austen, in *Northanger Abbey*

Memorable Passages:

On a Scale of 1 to 5 stars I rate this book as a solid _____

I POSTED A REVIEW OF THIS BOOK

Date posted:_____

Posted on:

☐ Amazon ☐ Goodreads ☐ Barnes & Noble ☐ Smashwords ☐ Kobo ☐ Alibris ☐ eBay

☐ Other websites: _____

Review:

Book Title [   ]

Author: _____ Publisher: _____

Publishing Date: _____ Edition: _____

☐ Paperback ☐ Hardcover ☐ eBook ☐ Audio Book ☐ comb or spiral bound

Pages [   ]   ☐ Fiction / Fiction Genre: _____

                         ☐ Nonfiction   ☐ Brand New   ☐ Pre-owned

Book Category or Subject: _____

Book was first introduced to me by _____

Book was acquired from _____ on (Date) _____

Date Started_____ Date Finished _____

Why do/did I want to read this book?_____

The book made me feel.... ☐ Inspired ☐ Engaged ☐ Happy ☐ Grateful

☐ Enthusiastic ☐ Fearful ☐ Sad ☐ Depressed ☐ Angry ☐ Melancholy

☐ Surprised ☐ Enchanted ☐ Satisfied ☐ Empty ☐ Wiser ☐_____

What I learned from this book:

What I liked about this book:	What I did not like about this book:	*Good friends, good books, and a sleepy conscience: this is the ideal life.* — Mark Twain

Memorable Passages:

On a Scale of 1 to 5 stars I rate this book as a solid _____

I POSTED A REVIEW OF THIS BOOK

Date posted:_____

Posted on:

☐ Amazon ☐ Goodreads ☐ Barnes & Noble ☐ Smashwords ☐ Kobo ☐ Alibris ☐ eBay

☐ Other websites: _____

Review:

Book Title

Author: _____ Publisher: _____

Publishing Date: _____ Edition: _____

☐ Paperback ☐ Hardcover ☐ eBook ☐ Audio Book ☐ comb or spiral bound

Pages [   ]   ☐ Fiction / Fiction Genre: _____

                       ☐ Nonfiction ☐ Brand New ☐ Pre-owned

Book Category or Subject: _____

Book was first introduced to me by _____

Book was acquired from _____ on (Date) _____

Date Started_____ Date Finished _____

Why do/did I want to read this book?_____

The book made me feel.... ☐ Inspired ☐ Engaged ☐ Happy ☐ Grateful

☐ Enthusiastic ☐ Fearful ☐ Sad ☐ Depressed ☐ Angry ☐ Melancholy

☐ Surprised ☐ Enchanted ☐ Satisfied ☐ Empty ☐ Wiser ☐_____

What I learned from this book:

What I liked about this book:

What I did not like about this book:

Where is human nature so weak as in the bookstore?
— Henry Ward Beecherr

Memorable Passages:

On a Scale of 1 to 5 stars I rate this book as a solid _____

I POSTED A REVIEW OF THIS BOOK

Date posted:_____

Posted on:

☐ Amazon ☐ Goodreads ☐ Barnes & Noble ☐ Smashwords ☐ Kobo ☐ Alibris ☐ eBay

☐ Other websites: _____

Review:

Book Title [   ]

Author: _____ Publisher: _____

Publishing Date: _____ Edition: _____

☐ Paperback ☐ Hardcover ☐ eBook ☐ Audio Book ☐ comb or spiral bound

Pages [   ]   ☐ Fiction / Fiction Genre: _____

                            ☐ Nonfiction ☐ Brand New ☐ Pre-owned

Book Category or Subject: _____

Book was first introduced to me by _____

Book was acquired from _____ on (Date) _____

Date Started_____ Date Finished _____

Why do/did I want to read this book?_____

The book made me feel.... ☐ Inspired ☐ Engaged ☐ Happy ☐ Grateful

☐ Enthusiastic ☐ Fearful ☐ Sad ☐ Depressed ☐ Angry ☐ Melancholy

☐ Surprised ☐ Enchanted ☐ Satisfied ☐ Empty ☐ Wiser ☐ _____

What I learned from this book:

What I liked about this book:	What I did not like about this book:	*What we become depends on what we read after all the professors have finished with us. The greatest university of all is the collection of books.* —Thomas Carlyle

Memorable Passages:

On a Scale of 1 to 5 stars I rate this book as a solid _____

I POSTED A REVIEW OF THIS BOOK

Date posted:_____

Posted on:

☐ Amazon ☐ Goodreads ☐ Barnes & Noble ☐ Smashwords ☐ Kobo ☐ Alibris ☐ eBay

☐ Other websites: _____

Review:

Book Title

Author: _____ Publisher: _____

Publishing Date: _____ Edition: _____

☐ Paperback ☐ Hardcover ☐ eBook ☐ Audio Book ☐ comb or spiral bound

Pages [   ]   ☐ Fiction / Fiction Genre: _____

                          ☐ Nonfiction   ☐ Brand New   ☐ Pre-owned

Book Category or Subject: _____

Book was first introduced to me by _____

Book was acquired from _____ on (Date) _____

Date Started_____ Date Finished _____

Why do/did I want to read this book?_____

The book made me feel.... ☐ Inspired ☐ Engaged ☐ Happy ☐ Grateful

☐ Enthusiastic ☐ Fearful ☐ Sad ☐ Depressed ☐ Angry ☐ Melancholy

☐ Surprised ☐ Enchanted ☐ Satisfied ☐ Empty ☐ Wiser ☐ _____

What I learned from this book:

What I liked about this book:

What I did not like about this book:

I have always imagined that paradise would always be a kind of library.
—Jorge Luis Borges

Memorable Passages:

On a Scale of 1 to 5 stars I rate this book as a solid _____

I POSTED A REVIEW OF THIS BOOK

Date posted:_____

Posted on:

☐ Amazon ☐ Goodreads ☐ Barnes & Noble ☐ Smashwords ☐ Kobo ☐ Alibris ☐ eBay

☐ Other websites: _____

Review:

Book Title

Author: _____ Publisher: _____

Publishing Date: _____ Edition: _____

☐ Paperback ☐ Hardcover ☐ eBook ☐ Audio Book ☐ comb or spiral bound

Pages [_____]   ☐ Fiction / Fiction Genre: _____

                          ☐ Nonfiction ☐ Brand New ☐ Pre-owned

Book Category or Subject: _____

Book was first introduced to me by _____

Book was acquired from _____ on (Date) _____

Date Started_____ Date Finished _____

Why do/did I want to read this book?_____

The book made me feel.... ☐ Inspired ☐ Engaged ☐ Happy ☐ Grateful

☐ Enthusiastic ☐ Fearful ☐ Sad ☐ Depressed ☐ Angry ☐ Melancholy

☐ Surprised ☐ Enchanted ☐ Satisfied ☐ Empty ☐ Wiser ☐ _____

> **What I learned from this book:**

What I liked about this book:	What I did not like about this book:	*Never lend books, for no one ever returns them; the Only books I have in by library are books thatother folk have lent me.* —Anatole France

Memorable Passages:

On a Scale of 1 to 5 stars I rate this book as a solid _____

I POSTED A REVIEW OF THIS BOOK

Date posted:_____

Posted on:

☐ Amazon ☐ Goodreads ☐ Barnes & Noble ☐ Smashwords ☐ Kobo ☐ Alibris ☐ eBay

☐ Other websites: _____

Review:

Book Title [   ]

Author: _____ Publisher: _____

Publishing Date: _____ Edition: _____

☐ Paperback ☐ Hardcover ☐ eBook ☐ Audio Book ☐ comb or spiral bound

Pages [   ]   ☐ Fiction / Fiction Genre: _____

☐ Nonfiction ☐ Brand New ☐ Pre-owned

Book Category or Subject: _____

Book was first introduced to me by _____

Book was acquired from _____ on (Date) _____

Date Started_____ Date Finished _____

Why do/did I want to read this book?_____

The book made me feel.... ☐ Inspired ☐ Engaged ☐ Happy ☐ Grateful

☐ Enthusiastic ☐ Fearful ☐ Sad ☐ Depressed ☐ Angry ☐ Melancholy

☐ Surprised ☐ Enchanted ☐ Satisfied ☐ Empty ☐ Wiser ☐ _____

What I learned from this book:

What I liked about this book:	What I did not like about this book:	*The best books for a man are not always those which the wise recommend, but often those which meet the peculiar wants, the natural thirst of his mind, and therefore awaken interest and rivet thought.* —William Ellery Channing

Memorable Passages:

On a Scale of 1 to 5 stars I rate this book as a solid _____

I POSTED A REVIEW OF THIS BOOK

Date posted:_____

Posted on:

☐ Amazon ☐ Goodreads ☐ Barnes & Noble ☐ Smashwords ☐ Kobo ☐ Alibris ☐ eBay

☐ Other websites: _____

Review:

Book Title

Author: _____ Publisher: _____

Publishing Date: _____ Edition: _____

☐ Paperback ☐ Hardcover ☐ eBook ☐ Audio Book ☐ comb or spiral bound

Pages [_____]   ☐ Fiction / Fiction Genre: _____

☐ Nonfiction   ☐ Brand New   ☐ Pre-owned

Book Category or Subject: _____

Book was first introduced to me by _____

Book was acquired from _____ on (Date) _____

Date Started _____ Date Finished _____

Why do/did I want to read this book? _____

The book made me feel.... ☐ Inspired ☐ Engaged ☐ Happy ☐ Grateful

☐ Enthusiastic ☐ Fearful ☐ Sad ☐ Depressed ☐ Angry ☐ Melancholy

☐ Surprised ☐ Enchanted ☐ Satisfied ☐ Empty ☐ Wiser ☐ _____

What I learned from this book:

What I liked about this book:

What I did not like about this book:

There is no friend as loyal as a book.
—Earnest Hemingway

Memorable Passages:

On a Scale of 1 to 5 stars I rate this book as a solid _____

I POSTED A REVIEW OF THIS BOOK

Date posted:_____
Posted on:

☐ Amazon ☐ Goodreads ☐ Barnes & Noble ☐ Smashwords ☐ Kobo ☐ Alibris ☐ eBay

☐ Other websites: _____

Review:

Book Title [   ]

Author: _____ Publisher: _____

Publishing Date: _____ Edition: _____

☐ Paperback ☐ Hardcover ☐ eBook ☐ Audio Book ☐ comb or spiral bound

Pages [   ]   ☐ Fiction / Fiction Genre: _____

                          ☐ Nonfiction   ☐ Brand New   ☐ Pre-owned

Book Category or Subject: _____

Book was first introduced to me by _____

Book was acquired from _____ on (Date) _____

Date Started_____ Date Finished _____

Why do/did I want to read this book?_____

The book made me feel.... ☐ Inspired ☐ Engaged ☐ Happy ☐ Grateful

☐ Enthusiastic ☐ Fearful ☐ Sad ☐ Depressed ☐ Angry ☐ Melancholy

☐ Surprised ☐ Enchanted ☐ Satisfied ☐ Empty ☐ Wiser ☐ _____

What I learned from this book:

What I liked about this book:

What I did not like about this book:

A man can never have too many books, too much red wine, or too much ammunition.
—Rudyard Kipling

Memorable Passages:

On a Scale of 1 to 5 stars I rate this book as a solid _____

I POSTED A REVIEW OF THIS BOOK

Date posted:_____

Posted on:

☐ Amazon ☐ Goodreads ☐ Barnes & Noble ☐ Smashwords ☐ Kobo ☐ Alibris ☐ eBay

☐ Other websites: _____

Review:

Book Title

Author: _____ Publisher: _____

Publishing Date: _____ Edition: _____

☐ Paperback ☐ Hardcover ☐ eBook ☐ Audio Book ☐ comb or spiral bound

Pages [   ]   ☐ Fiction / Fiction Genre: _____

                         ☐ Nonfiction   ☐ Brand New   ☐ Pre-owned

Book Category or Subject: _____

Book was first introduced to me by _____

Book was acquired from _____ on (Date) _____

Date Started_____ Date Finished _____

Why do/did I want to read this book?_____

The book made me feel.... ☐ Inspired ☐ Engaged ☐ Happy ☐ Grateful

☐ Enthusiastic ☐ Fearful ☐ Sad ☐ Depressed ☐ Angry ☐ Melancholy

☐ Surprised ☐ Enchanted ☐ Satisfied ☐ Empty ☐ Wiser ☐ _____

What I learned from this book:

What I liked about this book:

What I did not like about this book:

I'm old-fashioned and think that reading books is the most glorious pastime that humankind has yet devised.
—Wislawa Szymborka

Memorable Passages:

On a Scale of 1 to 5 stars I rate this book as a solid _____

I POSTED A REVIEW OF THIS BOOK

Date posted:_____
Posted on:

☐ Amazon ☐ Goodreads ☐ Barnes & Noble ☐ Smashwords ☐ Kobo ☐ Alibris ☐ eBay

☐ Other websites: _____

Review:

Book Title

Author: _____ Publisher: _____

Publishing Date: _____ Edition: _____

☐ Paperback ☐ Hardcover ☐ eBook ☐ Audio Book ☐ comb or spiral bound

Pages [   ]   ☐ Fiction / Fiction Genre: _____

                            ☐ Nonfiction ☐ Brand New ☐ Pre-owned

Book Category or Subject: _____

Book was first introduced to me by _____

Book was acquired from _____ on (Date) _____

Date Started_____ Date Finished _____

Why do/did I want to read this book?_____

The book made me feel.... ☐ Inspired ☐ Engaged ☐ Happy ☐ Grateful

☐ Enthusiastic ☐ Fearful ☐ Sad ☐ Depressed ☐ Angry ☐ Melancholy

☐ Surprised ☐ Enchanted ☐ Satisfied ☐ Empty ☐ Wiser ☐_____

What I learned from this book:

What I liked about this book:	What I did not like about this book:	*A retirement heaven is a well stocked library.* —M. Mitch Freeland

Memorable Passages:

On a Scale of 1 to 5 stars I rate this book as a solid _____

I POSTED A REVIEW OF THIS BOOK

Date posted:_____

Posted on:

☐ Amazon ☐ Goodreads ☐ Barnes & Noble ☐ Smashwords ☐ Kobo ☐ Alibris ☐ eBay

☐ Other websites: _____

Review:

Book Title

Author: _____ Publisher: _____

Publishing Date: _____ Edition: _____

☐ Paperback ☐ Hardcover ☐ eBook ☐ Audio Book ☐ comb or spiral bound

Pages [   ]   ☐ Fiction / Fiction Genre: _____

☐ Nonfiction   ☐ Brand New   ☐ Pre-owned

Book Category or Subject: _____

Book was first introduced to me by _____

Book was acquired from _____ on (Date) _____

Date Started_____ Date Finished _____

Why do/did I want to read this book?_____

The book made me feel.... ☐ Inspired ☐ Engaged ☐ Happy ☐ Grateful

☐ Enthusiastic ☐ Fearful ☐ Sad ☐ Depressed ☐ Angry ☐ Melancholy

☐ Surprised ☐ Enchanted ☐ Satisfied ☐ Empty ☐ Wiser ☐_____

What I learned from this book:

What I liked about this book:	What I did not like about this book:	*When you sell a man a book, you don't sell him 12 ounces of paper and ink and glue—you sell him a whole new life.* —Christopher Morley

Memorable Passages:

On a Scale of 1 to 5 stars I rate this book as a solid _____

I POSTED A REVIEW OF THIS BOOK

Date posted:_____

Posted on:

☐ Amazon ☐ Goodreads ☐ Barnes & Noble ☐ Smashwords ☐ Kobo ☐ Alibris ☐ eBay

☐ Other websites: _____

Review:

Book Title

Author: _____ Publisher: _____

Publishing Date: _____ Edition: _____

☐ Paperback ☐ Hardcover ☐ eBook ☐ Audio Book ☐ comb or spiral bound

Pages [_____]   ☐ Fiction / Fiction Genre: _____

☐ Nonfiction ☐ Brand New ☐ Pre-owned

Book Category or Subject: _____

Book was first introduced to me by _____

Book was acquired from _____ on (Date) _____

Date Started_____ Date Finished _____

Why do/did I want to read this book?_____

The book made me feel.... ☐ Inspired ☐ Engaged ☐ Happy ☐ Grateful

☐ Enthusiastic ☐ Fearful ☐ Sad ☐ Depressed ☐ Angry ☐ Melancholy

☐ Surprised ☐ Enchanted ☐ Satisfied ☐ Empty ☐ Wiser ☐ _____

What I learned from this book:

What I liked about this book:	What I did not like about this book:	*Inside every book is a journey of the most glorious kind—a journey that can be taken every time it is opened, and at anytime and at anyplace.* —M. Mitch Freeland

Memorable Passages:

On a Scale of 1 to 5 stars I rate this book as a solid _____

I POSTED A REVIEW OF THIS BOOK

Date posted:_____
Posted on:

☐ Amazon ☐ Goodreads ☐ Barnes & Noble ☐ Smashwords ☐ Kobo ☐ Alibris ☐ eBay

☐ Other websites: _____

Review:

Books I Have Lent

Title	Lent to	Date Lent	Date Returned

Books I Have Lent

Title	Lent to	Date Lent	Date Returned

Books I Have Borrowed

Title	Borrowed From	Date Borrowed	Date Returned

Books I Have Borrowed

Title	Borrowed From	Date Borrowed	Date Returned

Books I Have Gifted

Title	Gifted to	Date Gifted

Books I Have Gifted

Title	Gifted to	Date Gifted

100 Books I Want to Read

1._____

Date to Acquire _____

2._____

Date to Acquire _____

3._____

Date to Acquire _____

4._____

Date to Acquire _____

5._____

Date to Acquire _____

6._____

Date to Acquire _____

7._____

Date to Acquire _____

8._____

Date to Acquire _____

9._____

Date to Acquire _____

10._____

Date to Acquire _____

11._____

Date to Acquire _____

12._____

Date to Acquire _____

13._____

Date to Acquire _____

14._____

Date to Acquire _____

15._____

Date to Acquire _____

16._____

Date to Acquire _____

17._____

Date to Acquire _____

18._____

Date to Acquire _____

19._____

Date to Acquire _____

20._____

Date to Acquire _____

21._____

Date to Acquire _____

22._____

Date to Acquire _____

23._____

Date to Acquire _____

24._____

Date to Acquire _____

25._____

Date to Acquire _____

26._____

Date to Acquire _____

27._____

Date to Acquire _____

28._____

Date to Acquire _____

29._____

Date to Acquire _____

30._____

Date to Acquire _____

31._____

Date to Acquire _____

32._____

Date to Acquire _____

33._____

Date to Acquire _____

34._____

Date to Acquire _____

35._____

Date to Acquire _____

36._____

Date to Acquire _____

37._____

Date to Acquire _____

38._____

Date to Acquire _____

39._____

Date to Acquire _____

40._____

Date to Acquire _____

41._____

Date to Acquire _____

42._____

Date to Acquire _____

43._____

Date to Acquire _____

44._____

Date to Acquire _____

45._____

Date to Acquire _____

46._____

Date to Acquire _____

47._____

Date to Acquire _____

48._____

Date to Acquire _____

49._____

Date to Acquire _____

50._____

Date to Acquire _____

51._____

Date to Acquire _____

52._____

Date to Acquire _____

53._____

Date to Acquire _____

54._____

Date to Acquire _____

55._____

Date to Acquire _____

56._____

Date to Acquire _____

57._____

Date to Acquire _____

58._____

Date to Acquire _____

59._____

Date to Acquire _____

60._____

Date to Acquire _____

61._____

Date to Acquire _____

62._____

Date to Acquire _____

63._____

Date to Acquire _____

64._____

Date to Acquire _____

65._____

Date to Acquire _____

66._____

Date to Acquire _____

67._____

Date to Acquire _____

68._____

Date to Acquire _____

69._____

Date to Acquire _____

70._____

Date to Acquire _____

71._____

Date to Acquire _____

72._____

Date to Acquire _____

73._____

Date to Acquire _____

74._____

Date to Acquire _____

75._____

Date to Acquire _____

76._____

Date to Acquire _____

77._____

Date to Acquire _____

78._____

Date to Acquire _____

79._____

Date to Acquire _____

80._____

Date to Acquire _____

81._____

Date to Acquire _____

82._____

Date to Acquire _____

83._____

Date to Acquire _____

84._____

Date to Acquire _____

85._____

Date to Acquire _____

86._____

Date to Acquire _____

87._____

Date to Acquire _____

88._____

Date to Acquire _____

89._____

Date to Acquire _____

90._____

Date to Acquire _____

91._____

Date to Acquire _____

92._____

Date to Acquire _____

93._____

Date to Acquire _____

94._____

Date to Acquire _____

95._____

Date to Acquire _____

96._____

Date to Acquire _____

97._____

Date to Acquire _____

98._____

Date to Acquire _____

99._____

Date to Acquire _____

100._____

Date to Acquire _____

Books I Would Like to See on My Bookshelves

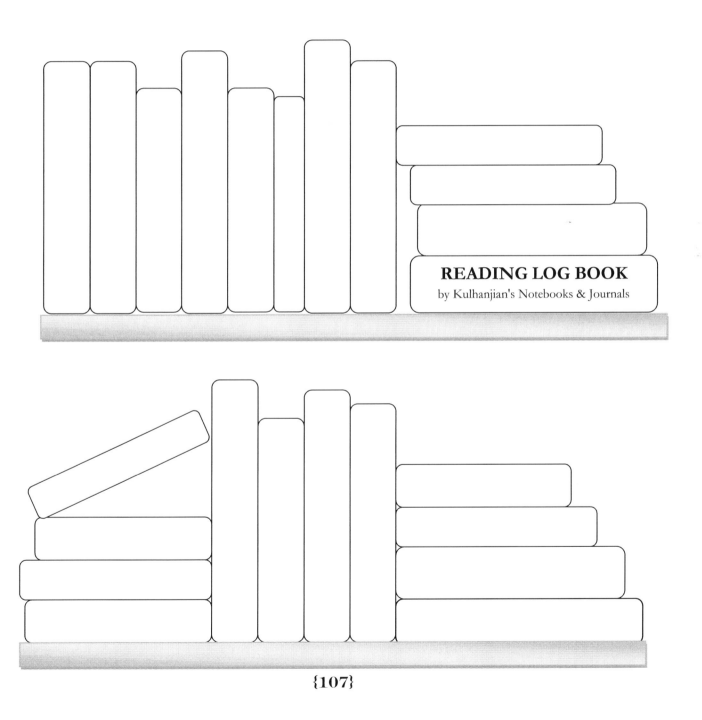

READING LOG BOOK
by Kulhanjian's Notebooks & Journals

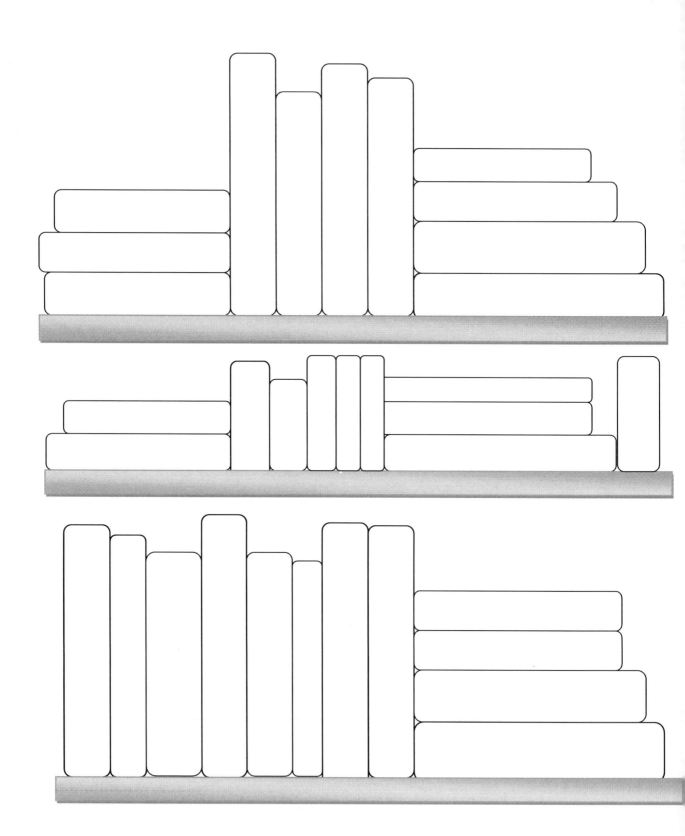

So Matilda's strong young mind continued to grow, nurtured by the voices of all those authors who had sent their books out into the world like ships on the sea. These books gave Matilda a hopeful and comforting message: You are not alone.
— Roald Dahl, in *Matilda*

Did you like this notebook? Was this notebook helpful?

Would you like to reorder?

Buy multiple books Direct and SAVE! Perfect for Book Clubs

MAKE IT A GIFT
Who do you know that loves to read?
A Reading Log Book makes a
thoughtful gift anytime

10 Reading Log Books for
only $64.99
FREE SHIPPING!

Visit us and discover the SAVINGS! It's Worth it.

Reorder Now at: **www.MitchFreeland.com**

Thank You
God Bless and See you soon.

M. Mitch Freeland

24915398R00071

Made in the USA
Lexington, KY
18 December 2018